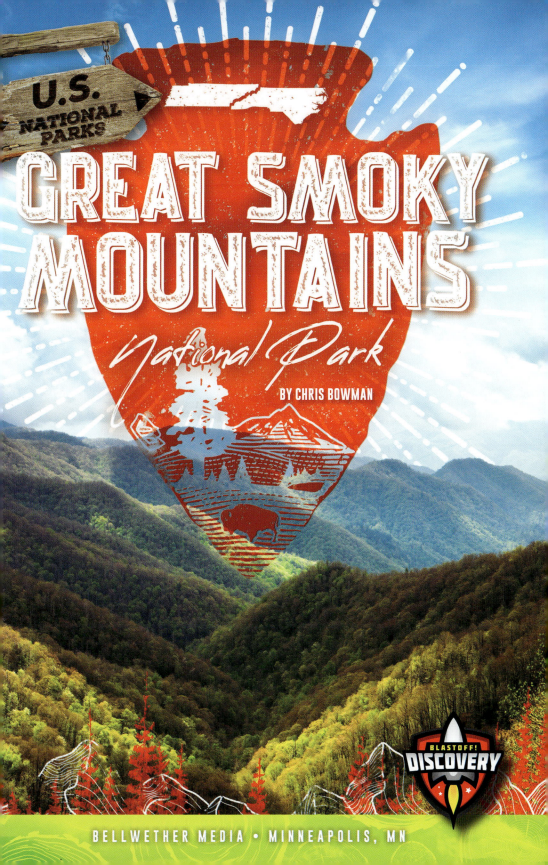

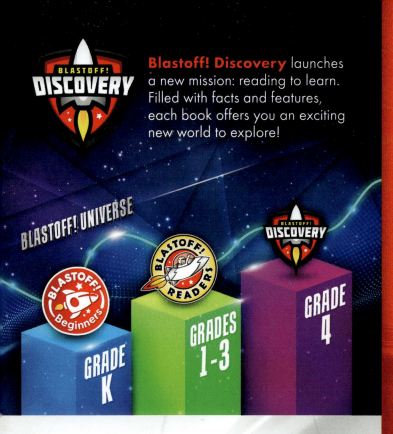

This edition first published in 2023 by Bellwether Media, Inc.

No part of this publication may be reproduced in whole or in part without written permission of the publisher.
For information regarding permission, write to Bellwether Media, Inc., Attention: Permissions Department,
6012 Blue Circle Drive, Minnetonka, MN 55343.

Library of Congress Cataloging-in-Publication Data

Names: Bowman, Chris, 1990- author.
Title: Great Smoky Mountains National Park / by Chris Bowman.
Description: Minneapolis : Bellwether Media, 2023 |
  Series: Blastoff! Discovery: U.S. national parks | Includes bibliographical references and index. | Audience: Ages 7-13 | Audience: Grades 4-6 |
  Summary: "Engaging images accompany information about Great Smoky Mountains National Park. The combination of high-interest subject matter and narrative text is intended for students in grades 3 through 8"–Provided by publisher.
Identifiers: LCCN 2022016485 (print) | LCCN 2022016486 (ebook) |
  ISBN 9781644877548 (library binding) | ISBN 9781648348006 (ebook)
Subjects: LCSH: Great Smoky Mountains National Park
  (N.C. and Tenn.)–Juvenile literature.
Classification: LCC F443.G7 B68 2023 (print) | LCC F443.G7 (ebook) |
  DDC 976.8/89–dc23/eng/20220413
LC record available at https://lccn.loc.gov/2022016485
LC ebook record available at https://lccn.loc.gov/2022016486

Text copyright © 2023 by Bellwether Media, Inc. BLASTOFF! DISCOVERY and associated logos are trademarks and/or registered trademarks of Bellwether Media, Inc.

Editor: Betsy Rathburn
Series Design: Jeffrey Kollock   Book Designer: Laura Sowers

Printed in the United States of America, North Mankato, MN.

TABLE OF CONTENTS

Clingmans Dome	4
Great Smoky Mountains National Park	6
The Land	8
Plants and Wildlife	12
Humans in Great Smoky Mountains National Park	16
Visiting Great Smoky Mountains National Park	22
Protecting the Park	24
Great Smoky Mountains National Park Facts	28
Glossary	30
To Learn More	31
Index	32

CLINGMANS DOME

RAINBOW FALLS

The air is warm and **humid** as a family begins their hike. They pass many large rocks and tree roots as the trail winds up through the forest and across streams. As they go higher, the trees open up to views of the mountains around them. Finally, the family reaches Rainbow Falls, where a thin veil of water falls 80 feet (24 meters) to the rocks below.

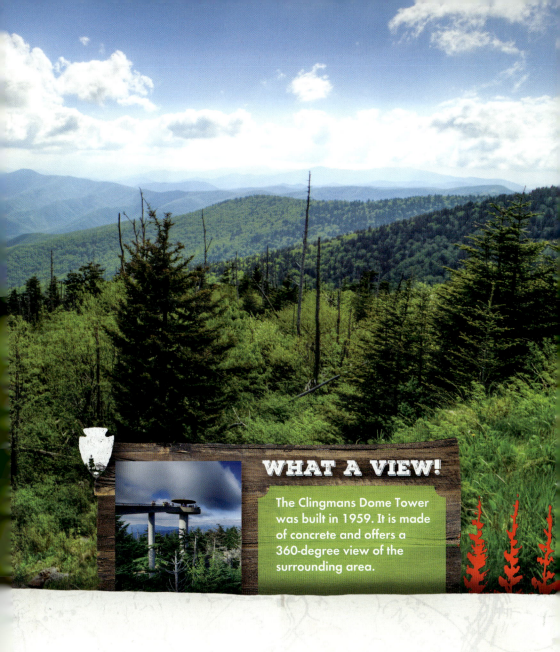

WHAT A VIEW!

The Clingmans Dome Tower was built in 1959. It is made of concrete and offers a 360-degree view of the surrounding area.

Later, the family drives to Clingmans Dome. They walk up to the **observation tower**. Forested mountains stretch out before them. They have an amazing view of Great Smoky Mountains National Park!

GREAT SMOKY MOUNTAINS NATIONAL PARK

Great Smoky Mountains National Park lies along the border between Tennessee and North Carolina. It covers 816 square miles (2,113 square kilometers) of forested mountains in these two states. These mountains are not actually smoky. They get their name from the fog that regularly covers the area.

Many visitors see the park by driving on Newfound Gap Road. The park is also home to around 70 miles (113 kilometers) of the **Appalachian Trail**. This popular section of the trail can take around one week to finish.

THE LAND

HIGH HEIGHTS

The Great Smokies are some of the tallest peaks of the Appalachian Mountains!

The Smoky Mountains began forming around 300 million years ago as **tectonic plates** smashed together. Pressure from this process pushed the land upward. This created the Appalachian Mountains. These are some of the oldest mountains in the world. They span nearly 2,000 miles (3,219 kilometers) across the eastern United States. The Great Smoky Mountains are a small area near the southern end of this range.

Over millions of years, **erosion** from wind and rain shaped the Smokies. This wore down mountain peaks and formed the area's valleys. Cycles of freezing and thawing caused further erosion. Water settled into cracks in rocks. When it froze, it expanded the cracks and broke the rocks. This led boulders to break off from mountain ledges.

HOW THE SMOKIES FORMED

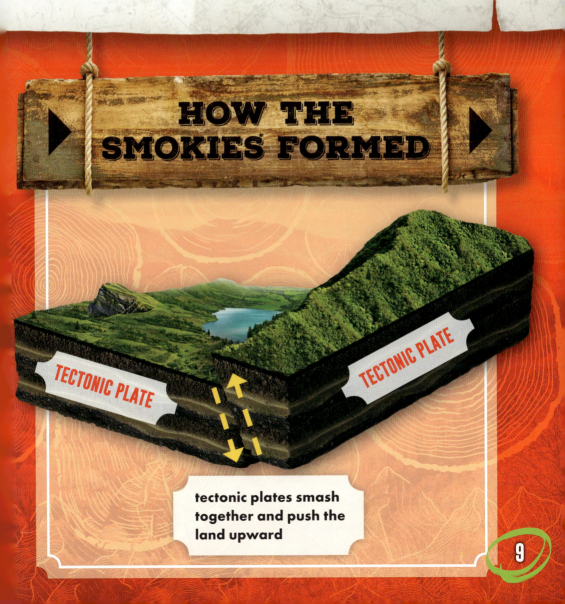

tectonic plates smash together and push the land upward

Almost all of the Great Smokies **ecosystem** is made up of forests. Hemlock trees grow throughout the park. Pine-oak forests are found in lower **elevations**. Slightly higher, northern hardwood forests are common. These trees give the park its beautiful fall colors! At the highest points in the park, spruce-fir forests are common.

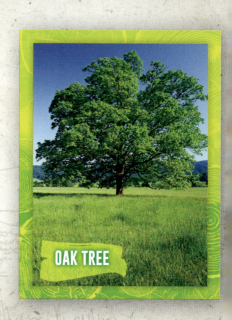

OAK TREE

AVERAGE TEMPERATURES

JANUARY
▲ HIGH: 35°F (2°C)
▼ LOW: 19°F (-7°C)

APRIL
▲ HIGH: 49°F (9°C)
▼ LOW: 34°F (1°C)

JULY
▲ HIGH: 65°F (18°C)
▼ LOW: 53°F (12°C)

OCTOBER
▲ HIGH: 53°F (12°C)
▼ LOW: 38°F (3°C)

°F = degrees Fahrenheit   °C = degrees Celsius

   The park has four seasons. Summer is warm, while spring and fall are cool. Winter brings big snowstorms to higher elevations. Rain is common throughout the year. The highest elevations get the most rain. Some peaks receive 85 inches (216 centimeters) of rain each year!

PLANTS AND WILDLIFE

The Great Smoky Mountains are home to many kinds of plants and animals. The vast forests are a perfect home for black bears. Coyotes and bobcats also hide among the trees. Elk and white-tailed deer are often seen in the park. Smaller mammals such as opossums, skunks, and foxes are common in the area.

Northern saw-whet owls watch over spruce forests high in the mountains. In lower areas, eastern screech owls search for insects and small mammals. Bats fly out of the park's caves at dusk. In May and June, **synchronous** fireflies light up the night.

WHITE-TAILED DEER

BOBCAT

RED FOX

NORTHERN SAW-WHET OWL

LITTLE BROWN BAT

The park's streams are filled with fish. **Native** brook trout are common. Two other kinds of trout have also been brought to the area. There are many salamander species in the Smokies. Lungless salamanders are often found near the park's streams. Frogs and toads hop among them.

BROOK TROUT

DWARF IRISES

A WILD PLACE

The park is one of the largest wilderness areas in the eastern United States!

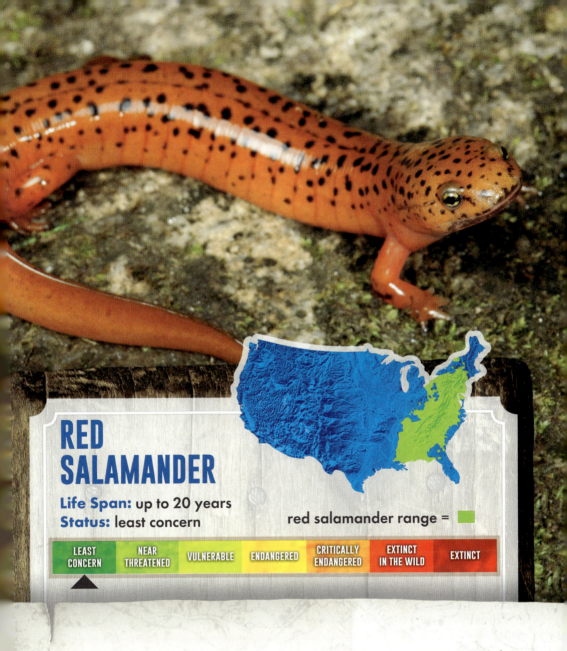

RED SALAMANDER

Life Span: up to 20 years
Status: least concern

red salamander range =

| LEAST CONCERN | NEAR THREATENED | VULNERABLE | ENDANGERED | CRITICALLY ENDANGERED | EXTINCT IN THE WILD | EXTINCT |

Lizards such as the eastern slender glass lizard live in forested areas at lower elevations. Eastern box turtles are also common in lower forests. The park's meadows and **balds** are filled with grasses and shrubs. Spring and summer bring wildflowers such as dwarf irises, cardinal flowers, and goldenrods into bloom.

HUMANS IN GREAT SMOKY MOUNTAINS NATIONAL PARK

People have called the Great Smoky Mountains home for more than 12,000 years. At first, hunters and gatherers passed through the area. Around 1,000 years ago, the Cherokee people made homes in the area. The Cherokee people lived in small communities in **fertile** valleys. They hunted and farmed the land. They also traded with nearby communities.

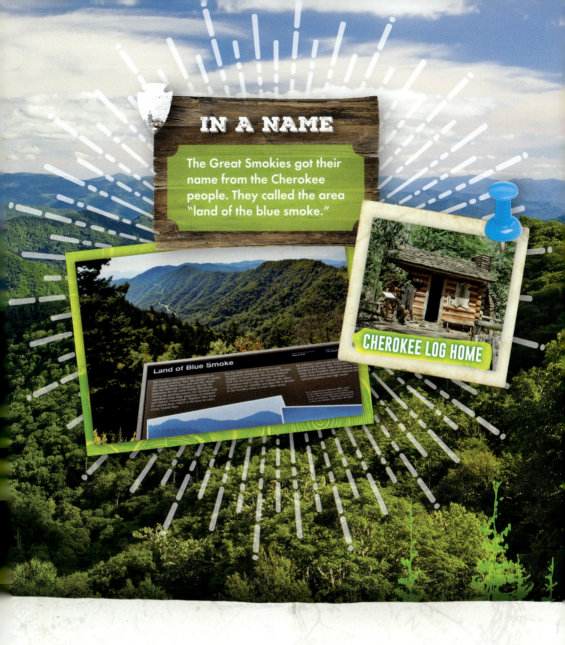

IN A NAME

The Great Smokies got their name from the Cherokee people. They called the area "land of the blue smoke."

CHEROKEE LOG HOME

White settlers moved into the area in the 1700s. They built farms and lived in log homes and cabins. Small communities centered around churches and schools. By the early 1800s, Cherokee communities adopted farming and building practices from these newcomers.

The U.S. government forced the Cherokee people to move from the Great Smokies in the late 1830s. Thousands of Cherokee people were forced to move west to Arkansas and Oklahoma. This event has become known as the **Trail of Tears**.

Some Cherokee people were allowed to remain in the area. Today, they are known as the Eastern Band of the Cherokee Indians. Many live in the Qualla Boundary, just outside of Great Smoky Mountains National Park in North Carolina.

TRAIL OF TEARS

A PLACE TO LEARN

The Museum of the Cherokee Indian is located near the park in Cherokee, North Carolina. The museum offers visitors many ways to learn about Cherokee art and history.

The Great Smokies were heavily logged in the early 1900s. Many people wanted to protect the area from further damage. In the 1920s, the U.S. government began the process of establishing a national park. But many people still lived in the Smoky Mountains. The government had to buy the land from farmers and other landowners.

Most families had to leave the area. Some were allowed to stay behind. Today, their log homes and buildings are protected by the park. Great Smoky Mountains National Park was established in 1934. It was **dedicated** by President Franklin Delano Roosevelt in 1940.

PRESIDENT FRANKLIN DELANO ROOSEVELT

VISITING GREAT SMOKY MOUNTAINS NATIONAL PARK

Great Smoky Mountains National Park offers something for every visitor. Those interested in history can visit the park's collection of historic buildings. Visitors can stop by houses, churches, and mills to see how early communities lived in the area.

MILL

HORSEBACK RIDING

TOP SITES

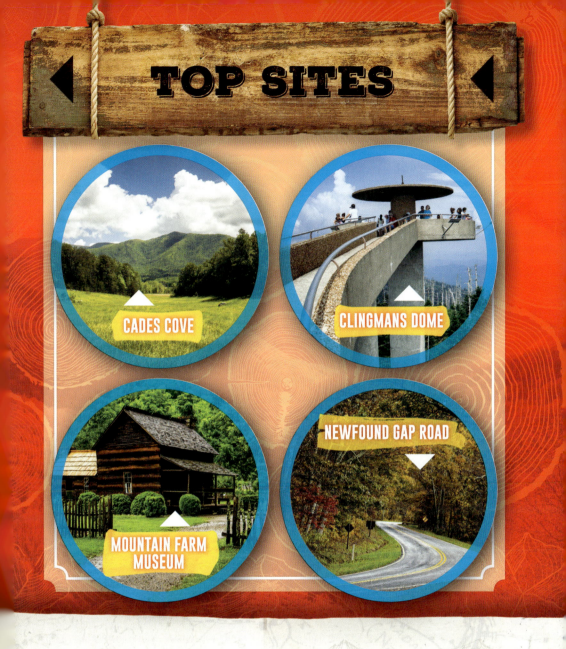

CADES COVE

CLINGMANS DOME

MOUNTAIN FARM MUSEUM

NEWFOUND GAP ROAD

Hiking is popular in the park. There are around 800 miles (1,300 kilometers) of trails. Horseback rides and scenic drives are other favorite ways to see the park's beautiful views. Mountain streams are favorite places for fishing. The vast forests of the Smokies are also great for bird-watching.

PROTECTING THE PARK

Great Smoky Mountains is the most visited national park in the U.S. The crowds that drive to the Smokies affect the park in a variety of ways. Hiking can cause erosion if people leave the trails. This harms plant and animal **habitats**.

Cars pollute the air, which also harms plants and animals in the area. **Acid rain** from pollution hurts streams and forests. Air pollution also affects visitors to the park. **Visibility** in the mountains has gotten worse in recent years. People are not able to see as far or as well as they used to.

CARS ON CADES COVE LOOP ROAD

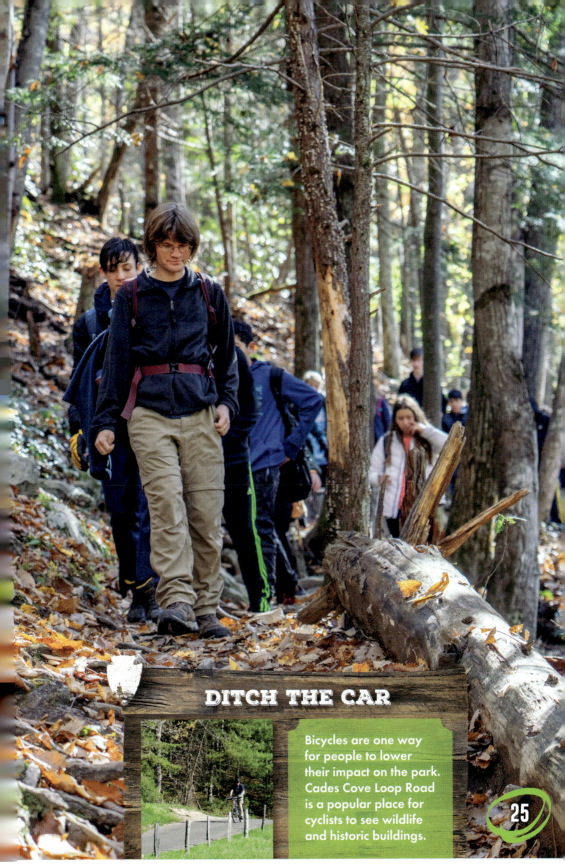

DITCH THE CAR

Bicycles are one way for people to lower their impact on the park. Cades Cove Loop Road is a popular place for cyclists to see wildlife and historic buildings.

25

Visitors can help protect the Great Smokies. Staying on the trails and picking up trash helps keep the forests safe. Electric and **fuel-efficient** cars limit air pollution from driving through the park. Less pollution means cleaner air, water, and soil for the park's wildlife.

People can also help the Smokies by reducing **climate change**. Warming temperatures threaten many of the park's native plants and animals. If we all do our part, future visitors can enjoy the wonder of the Great Smokies!

GREAT SMOKY MOUNTAINS NATIONAL PARK FACTS

Area: **816** square miles (2,113 square kilometers)

Area Rank: **19**TH largest park

Date Established: June 15, 1934

Annual Visitors: 14.1 million visitors in 2021

Population Rank: **1**ST most visited park in 2021

Highest point: Clingmans Dome; 6,643 feet (2,025 meters)

TIMELINE

1830s
Most of the Cherokee people are forced to move west by the U.S. government

EARLY 1900s
Heavy logging threatens the area's natural habitats

1920s
The government begins the process of purchasing land for the park

28

FOOD WEB

BOBCAT

EASTERN COTTONTAIL RABBIT

WOOD DUCK

BLACK HUCKLEBERRIES

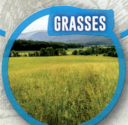
GRASSES

MAYFLY LARVA

1934
Great Smoky Mountains National Park is established

1959
The Clingmans Dome Tower is built

acid rain—rainfall that has been made acidic by pollution

Appalachian Trail—a hiking trail from Georgia to Maine; the Appalachian Trail is about 2,200 miles (3,541 kilometers) long.

balds—grassy areas on mountains

climate change—a human-caused change in Earth's weather due to warming temperatures

dedicated—formally opened to the public

ecosystem—a community of living things that includes plants, animals, and the environments around them

elevations—heights above sea level

erosion—the process through which rocks are worn away by wind, water, or ice

fertile—able to support growth

fuel-efficient—able to use less fuel

habitats—natural homes of plants and animals

humid—having a lot of moisture in the air

native—originally from the area or having begun in the area

observation tower—a place to see things far in the distance

synchronous—happening at the same time; synchronous fireflies often light up at the same time.

tectonic plates—large pieces of the earth's crust

Trail of Tears—the forced relocation of up to 100,000 Native Americans from their homelands to areas farther west in the 1830s; about 15,000 people died on the journey.

visibility—the amount that a person can see into the distance, usually based on light and conditions

TO LEARN MORE

AT THE LIBRARY

Gregory, Josh. *Great Smoky Mountains*. New York, N.Y.: Children's Press, 2018.

Payne, Stefanie. *The National Parks: Discover All 62 Parks of the United States*. New York, N.Y.: DK Publishing, 2020.

Sommer, Nathan. *North Carolina*. Minneapolis, Minn.: Bellwether Media, 2022.

ON THE WEB

FACTSURFER

Factsurfer.com gives you a safe, fun way to find more information.

1. Go to www.factsurfer.com.

2. Enter "Great Smoky Mountains National Park" into the search box and click 🔍.

3. Select your book cover to see a list of related content.

INDEX

activities, 6, 19, 22–23, 25
Appalachian Mountains, 8
Appalachian Trail, 6
average temperatures, 11
Cades Cove Loop Road, 24, 25
Cherokee, 16, 17, 18, 19
climate, 11
climate change, 27
Clingmans Dome, 4–5
fast facts, 28–29
formation, 8, 9
history, 5, 16, 17, 18, 20, 21, 22
landscape, 4, 5, 6, 8, 9, 10, 12, 14, 15, 16, 23
location, 6, 8
map, 6
Museum of the Cherokee Indian, 19
name, 6, 17

Newfound Gap Road, 6, 7
North Carolina, 6, 18, 19
people, 16, 17, 18, 19, 20, 21
plants, 10, 12, 14, 15, 24, 27
pollution, 24, 26
protecting the park, 24, 25, 26, 27
Qualla Boundary, 18
Rainbow Falls, 4
Roosevelt, Franklin Delano, 21
size, 6, 14
Tennessee, 6
threats, 24
top sites, 23
wildlife, 12, 13, 14, 15, 23, 24, 25, 26, 27

The images in this book are reproduced through the courtesy of: Dave Allen Photography, cover, pp. 23 (Cades Cove), 26-27; CrackerClips Stock Media, p. 3; Theron Stripling III, pp. 4 (Rainbow Falls), 29 (1959); Simon Crumpton/ Alamy, pp. 4-5; Zoonar GmbH/ Alamy, p. 5 (Clingmans Dome); anthony heflin, pp. 6-7; Jon Bilous, p. 7 (Newfoundland Gap Road); Steven Milligan, p. 8; William Manning/ Alamy, p. 10 (oak tree); (c) Sean Board, p. 10; Nickolay Khoroshkov, p. 11; Jake Daugherty, p. 12 (white-tailed deer); Don Mammoser, pp. 12 (bobcat), 29 (bobcat); Rudmer Zwerver, p. 12 (red fox); FotoRequest, p. 12 (northern saw-whet owl); William Wise, p. 12 (little brown bat); critterbiz, p. 13; COULANGES, p. 14 (brook trout); Daniel Dempster Photography/ Alamy, pp. 14 (dwarf irises), 25 (bicycles); Nathan A Shepard, p. 15; Christopher Aquino, pp. 16-17; Jennifer Wright/ Alamy, p. 17 (Land of Blue Smoke); North Wind Picture Archive, p. 17 (Cherokee log home); Picture History/ Newscom, pp. 18, 28 (1830s); kurdistan, pp. 18-19; ehrlif/ Alamy, p. 19 (Museum of Cherokee Indian); Weidman Photography, p. 20; Vincenzo Laviosa/ Wikipedia, p. 21 (President Franklin Delano Roosevelt); JACK ARNOUTS, p. 21; Jonathan Ross, p. 22 (mill); Michele Burgess/ Alamy, p. 22 (horseback riding); smartstock, p. 23 (Clingmans Dome); ESB Professional, p. 23 (Mountain Farm Museum); Thomas Gari, p. 23 (Newfoundland Gap Road); Pat Canova/ Alamy, p. 24 (cars); jadimages, pp. 24-25, 29 (1934); Pat & Chuck Blackley/ Alamy, p. 27; starryvoyage, pp. 28-29, 30-31, 32; State Archives of North Carolina/ Wikipedia, p. 28 (early 1900s); str946/ Wikipedia, p. 28 (1920s); ArCaLu, p. 29 (eastern cottontail); Nick Pecker, p. 29 (wood duck); Julija Ogrodowski, p. 29 (black huckleberries); Zack Frank, p. 29 (grasses); tartmany, p. 29 (mayfly larva); Francis Bossé, p. 31.